Brink

Also by Charlotte Clutterbuck
Soundings, Five Islands Press, 1997
Encounters with God in Medieval and Early Modern Poetry, Ashgate, 2005
Ion, Piccolo Press, 2012
Shift Control, Picaro Poets, 2017

Charlotte Clutterbuck

Brink

PICARO PRESS

Acknowledgements

Special thanks to Varuna for awarding me three fellowships, ACTArts for financial support, Round Table Poets and Wollongong Poetry Workshop, Deb Westbury and Susan Hampton.

Many of these poems have been previously published in *Nightjar* (Newcastle Poetry Prize Anthology, 1997), *Blue Dog, The Night Road* (Newcastle Poetry Prize Anthology, 2009) *Eureka St, Meanjin, Canberra Times, FourW, Holding Patterns* (Science Week Anthology, 2010), *Mascara, Poetrix, The Attitude of Cups* (ed. Sue Stanford, MPU, 2011), *Ion* (Piccolo Press, 2012), *Women at Work* (ed. Libby Hathorn, 2012).

Winner, Romanos the Melodist Prize for Religious Poetry, 2002. David Campbell Prize, 2009.

Brink
ISBN 978 1 921691 60 7
Copyright © text Charlote Clutterbuck 2012
Cover image © US Department of the Interior, 1977
Wheeling Suspension Bridge

First published by Picaro Press 2012

This edition published 2022 by
Picaro Press – an imprint of

GINNINDERRA PRESS
PO Box 3461 Port Adelaide 5015
www.ginninderrapress.com.au

Contents

I: Compass
To Speak of the Good that Is in Marriage	11
Metamorphic	12
Restless	13
Inland Flight	14
Contrasts	15
Compass	17
Mum's Not the Word	19

II: Gravity
Momentum	23
On Being Asked to Write an Enigmatic Poem	24
Conversation	25
Complex Horizons	26
Gravity	33
Compound Tenses	36

III: Uncertainty Principle
Husbandry	41
Sticky Wicket	42
Station	44
Uncertainty Principle	46
Wordless	47

IV: Jarred
Jarred	51
Flat Earth	53
Unsettled	55
Tricky Arithmetic	57
Ordinary Time	60
Responses	63
Infidelities	64

V: Translated

Because	69
Just My Cup of Tea	70
Why I Still Go to Church	73
Found in Translation	75
Stolen Lines	77
Chapel in Languedoc	78
If	80
Depth of Field	81
Whatness	82
Code to Found in Translation	83

If you try to run away from it, if you are scared to go to the brink, you are lost… We walked to the brink and we looked it in the face.

> John Foster Dulles

Morning, at the brown brink eastward, springs –
> Gerard Manley Hopkins

I: Compass

To Speak of the Good that Is in Marriage

Someone to carry my skis when there was no snow
and wait when I couldn't keep up

someone to kill blue-tongue lizards
half-dismembered by the Jack Russells

whack the brown snake with an axe
as it rustled down the drain by the garage

someone to act out the villains while I read
(Uriah's wringing hands, Carker's terrifying teeth)

to share nights when our son had whooping cough
and cry when he started school

to build him a fort, to be bashed
by nephews with light-sabres

to patch leaking roofs and service the car
and be desolate when my father died

to rehang my mother's doors
change beds full of vomit in the night

to bring flowers for our daughter's thresholds
eat the marmalade I was saving for later

to razz up our grandson till he can't sleep
and ogle the last helping of pie

to screech along with radio sopranos
to be sensible when I wasn't.

Metamorphic

Cow Bay

Twenty-five years – no space
for his wood, my books. We dig
through clay so he can build a room
for each (baulking for six months
at raising the wall between)

and when mine's done, except the lights
he travels alone, sees whales lift
from icy seas, sails from Cape Horn
to the still-seething crater
of Deception Island, and comes home.

In my turn, I go north
to dead volcanoes, rainforest edging sea.
Our two pieces of Gondwana, separate forever
keep the same record, in fossils
under ice, in living fig and fern.

The sun's fire burns on leaping water-drops
waves scour into silt these rocks
laid down by silt, heated and bent into folds.
Feet in wet soil, body damp with rain
words a waterfall I harvest with my fingers.

When I return, two globes reflect
and catch each other's glow
from both my windows, until a chain of lights
hangs side-by-side in the darkening
winter branches of the trees outside.

Restless

The wife knew
there was somewhere beyond.

Her heart was a kite
tugging her feet
he was the anchor
she a sail flapping.

She remembered two goats
chained together in a paddock
one eating the grass, the other
stubbornly trying to get
through the fence.

When they planted
two Manchurian pears
at the gate
one flourished
the other was stunted

when they knocked old bricks
out of the wall
there was a jagged space

there was the sky.

Inland Flight

Leaving the damp, rich warmth of the coast
I fly over arid mountains, barely tinged
with green, reading the map of this vast country.

In the same distance as Land's End to Graves End
these roads lead to no houses, no crops
no horizon, only a merging of dusty earth and sky.

Someone has been shaking out the rivers' ropes
painting the marbled endpapers of soil with creeks
combing the earth's wet hair, and plaiting it over her breast

flicking from his fingers the shining drops of lakes
towards Mount Isa, where the grooved hills rise
through evening's grey like blankets on a rumpled bed

and, with a last juggler's gesture, God
spins up the silver ball of the moon in the indigo haze
and catches the red-hazed sun in the indigo hills of his hand.

Contrasts

Field trip with indigenous students

Hermannsburg – white faces
selling tapes of black women's voices
singing Lutheran hymns in the Arrernte tongue

the Catholic Mission which pays
for stolen children with plastic rosary beads
a crucified shiny Christ who opens and shuts
his eyes as the viewer moves

the glamour and glitter of the casino
dark fingers feeding stacks
of golden coins into idols
the spiritual gestures of the croupier

but also, zebra finches, spinifex pigeons
the curved backs of the Caterpillar Ranges
the sun's light softening over the Gap.

*

As we walk round the Rock's brooding potency
something turns my one close shot
into a blank negative, shrugs off
the body of a reckless climber.

Outside our bus there is silence.
As dawn wakens the Olgas
some of us who've lost their traditions
chiack and pop flashes like tourists.

But you, woman of the Uin nation
speak little, walk slowly, wait
for the guidance of butterflies.

Blood mixed, language mostly lost, still
you're strong in the lore of eastern shores
your sea-grey eyes washed
by the rhythms of this inland sea.

The Olgas' female-seeming form
is Kata Tjuta, sacred to men.
You will not walk there, but leave me to choose.

We walk elsewhere – Not here, you warn me
here men worked stones, here the wind's voice
forbids us to sit, but here we may rest
in the bell of the pun-pun-punula bird.

Compass

Mt Nakadake, Aso-san

On the map it looked innocent
but suddenly I found myself

cowering, halfway up the rim
of the volcano, too scared to think

creeping up the slippery bare spine
leaving far below the wisp of smoking sulphur

leaning left towards a slide down scree
that would break just arms and legs

unable to look right at the plunge
clutching the compass he gave me.

On the first peak a couple answered
their mobile, moshi moshi.

Crawling round the brink of the crater
I found a gentler slope

above the green folds of the caldera
could eat without terror of a shifting rock

scramble down a watercourse
where a fall would only sprain a knee.

Then I could breathe and cross
the lunar plain of ash

and the wind caught
in a little hollow with a sigh

a buffet, a bluster over
the autumn's sunlit grassheads.

Mum's Not the Word

For thirty years
in her home, on holidays
known only as

Mum-where's-my-toothbrush
Mum-where's-the-toilet
Ask-Mum-what's-for-dinner…

> Mums become inexplicably afraid
> of horses, heights, cars
> railway stations and public toilets.
>
> Rarely in this present moment
> always slightly on edge
> looking behind, ahead, at their watches
>
> even when out, Mums have to be back
> to cook dinner, take in the washing
> provision their children for expeditions.
>
> Mums, when necessary,
> put children before themselves
> almost always before their husbands

But now that they've grown up
Mum wants her name back

the one she was given
before anyone knew who she was

and Mum wants a nickname
that acknowledges who I've become.

II: Gravity

II: Gravity

Momentum

Moments in a café
words only half understood
a feeling recognised
only by one
a scrawled address
kept in a wallet, nine years

a tentative greeting
touch of hands
green grapes, a cup
shoulders ploughing blue water
bar-tailed godwits flown
from Siberia non-stop
to this sandbar.

You give me a name.

Hush of waves on the shore
the lights of the city
beside the point
cool sand under bare feet
brown shard of glass
blood on path, on towel

a question taken the wrong way
answered the right
in the blink of a thought
utterly changed
not knowing how deep
your eyes were
till I plunged.

On Being Asked to Write an Enigmatic Poem

no subject, no object, no cause or effect
no attempt to finalise, refine, define, confine
no questions, no answers, no statements, no facts
not even any similes or metaphors to yoke
meanings by violence together
no proverbs, maxims, and definitely no clichés
maybe paradoxes, oxymorons, and quibbling
but no interventions from the author
no juxtapositions jockeying for position
no metonyms or synechdoches
even negative capability
is barred, along with objective correlatives
intertextuality and classical or Shakespearean allusions
and precious words like tintinnabulation
but above all
absolutely no
mention of
God.

Conversation

You ask me about Ordinary Time

It's the green time of most chasubles
infuses the ordinary time
between Pentecost and Advent
with nothing-special daily observance.

Sometimes, you said
in your ordinary life
a prayer will arise
make it more cohesive.

You wouldn't have known
about the god-spot without drugs.

I knew from sunsets
and restlessness
a sort of ache
insistent

that you felt in the interior
of cadences
and teaching the sequence of the mass
as a perfect narrative arc.

Complex Horizons

At Varuna

Dawkins would say I'm deluded
collaborating with you on a book about God
two in cahoots
(French: *cahute*, 'hut or cabin')
in a world unhoused, split between

those who think they know everything

those who think they know there is nothing.

How, in this combative weather, are those
who stumble willingly on
to navigate between
godlessness and overgodliness, beyond
preaching, blasphemy, debate
into a conversation, where two so different
voices might resolve
domination into cadence?

*

At the same time, I'm wrestling with form.
How to write my father's life seven years after his death
without the pen's brutal incisions
how to shape a narrative whose submarine-combat climax
peaked too early, how to list
his too-many talents without listing
steer between hagiography and warts-and-all?

Is that why, since he died, I've been inflicted with warts
every poem stuck in the doldrums
the marriage of form and content needing counselling?

*

I walk in a fog at Katoomba
pleased with myself
for not being disappointed
about not seeing sunrise on cliffs
for being able to perceive
shifts of water and light
how various and clear
sounds drip and splash
how rich the green-bice
and vermillion
when vision is quietened
by absence of sunlight

noticing how observant I am
of black-chinned honeyeaters and limandra
I slip on the wet metal steps
to the Three Sisters

wrench my shoulders
and the experience
into regular stanzas.

*

I'm looking over the rails at an idiot
on a ledge halfway down Katoomba Falls
looking over the drop

decide to rewrite a bad poem backwards
open a box you sent me
words clipped from newspapers
juxtapose at random
surprise yourself.

When I lose momentum
in my backwards journey
to convey how it feels
to encounter a vision
four dark hands
over a dinner table
saying what mattered
while Helmut and I
translated only the words
that were unnecessary
from the moment when
I and the Walpeyankere woman
stood in a breezeway in Alice Springs
and saw the tall German husband
with his cloud of angel hair
overshadowed by his six-foot-two wife
an African dancer, descending the stairs
hooking us with her smile

I sift words from the box
complex   horizons
but still beat
the lines into regularity.

*

Next morning, I take a young journalist walking.
She's been to a barbecue
in Libya, but never walked in the bush.
She's intrepid in Baghdad
and Beirut, but her shoes
are white and soft.
She says, *Someone is lost
in the mountains.*

I say, *This is a fire-trail
if you want to step off
and get lost, I suppose you could.*
I shoulder my Tintin pack with the food
water, space blanket
we'd need if we did get lost.

She asks too many questions.
I give far too many answers
including that my doctorate
was about how poets encounter God.

She asks if I am religious and I babble
but I never pray for anyone to be converted
am gobsmacked when she says, *I do*
turns out to be a sweet fundamentalist, shocked
by Islamic fundamentalism.

She gives me Popper's critique
of scientific positivism
to use in the God-Book

her jaw and throat look stiff
from the strain
of her complex horizons.

*

After too many steps and words
I ring a healer at random.
She says, *If you can come right now*
knees indicate problems with direction.

Energies realign, her hands feel like yours.

I take the afternoon slowly
waiting to be directed
tinker at the edges of poems
fling seven years' worth onto the floor.

Trashing them would cut a limb
from my narrative
but the evidence is there on the carpet

form strangling content.

Happy to see the problem even if I can't
work out the answer, I ring
you sound so bleak
*Twenty years' work, forcing myself
through, I just want it off my desk.*

In our different towns we light candles
ask the work what it wants
go for a walk, a swim
let what happens, happen.

In sweet, bright dreams
I let go the wing's strut
without a parachute
a bumpy, painless landing.

In the morning, something I've never done
a long bath
perfect shape, perfect heat.

Leaving the poems spreadeagled
on the floor until they call
eating breakfast in the sunny autumn garden
I remember that my father
surprised me into stanzas
about the lacks and love in him.

If he led me into form, he could
(despite his jibes at chopped-up prose)
lead me out of it.

Stepping across the garden, I'm stopped
at the door, so strong
his presence, so him, so changed
raised a spiritual body.

That night, I light a bonfire of lyrics
sacrifice form and rest content.

Gravity

>Quark:
>a question mark
>a hypothetical particle
>(dialect, in *Finnegan's Wake*): to caw or croak

If the earth rises
infinitesimally to meet
my foot as I run
along the escarpment
where Mt Solitary rises
from the early-morning fog

while a gaggle of white cockies
launch themselves for zest
into the valley, squarking

and a pair of black cockatoos
mutter gravely
in a bluegum
about hoi polloi
and fly primly away

then I exert a pull
on every other body
in the universe
even Saiph and Rigel
the knees of Orion
or your hand curled
next to mine on the table.

As a radio telescope
picks up the hum
from the far side
of Aldebaran, your star

and astronomers listen
to the bass notes
of a black hole
take the measure
of a quark's pulse

I feel your murmured
prayer against my heart
your steadying hand
on my chest. You draw out
my ideas, massage
the knots from my back
give me a ride
in your wheelbarrow.

I finish the wine
from your glass
take you to Mass
stroke back
your springy hair.

Almost timidly
you ask how I
can be good to you?

What else can I do
when the light from Antares
took six million years
to reach my pupil
as I hold you steady
on the station platform
your voice subzero
with interstellar space.

Compound Tenses

Simple past

> you saw the ring
> on my finger
>
> I was afraid
> what did you want?
>
> I never rang
> I never passed through your town.

Imperfect insects
born to form the angelic butterfly

> I was almost forgetting
> you were waiting.

Perfect love casts out fear

> nine years later
> you said, we've met before.

You had already loved me with a pluperfect love.

The future is tense

> we will never live together.

There's no simple present

but even if grammatical rules
have to coldly split
us like infinitives
this is the future perfect

                    we will have loved each other.

III: Uncertainty Principle

Husbandry

There's husbandry in heaven: their candles are all out.
— Shakespeare, *Macbeth*

Some toad has bought the kid
next door a mini-bike
noisy miners are in spring bloom
I'm out in the paddock
poisoning the Bridal Veil
remembering the skies
spoonbills and pelicans.

He's gone to work for thirty years
cleaned out the gutters
built me floor-to-ceiling bookshelves

but our car has a screw or two loose
we let maintenance get overdue
the timing chain has fallen into the engine
and one tyre's deflated.
Don't ride on the rim
he said last time I had a puncture
elementary physics.

To uproot myself
is to leave the earth
empty beside him.

To stay is to lop off my branches
and even then not enough space
for the slow growth
of his fine-grained hardwood.

Last one put out the lights.

Sticky Wicket

He was stuck – struck by a bolt
from the blue – was I steadfast
or stuckfast – defending my wicket
with irritability or stickability
stuck in the mud – toad in the hole
blind as a mole – I was a stickler
I thought I was a sticker – staking
plants up with pea-sticks
listening for frogs in the pond
for peace where the cricket sings
mind in a fog – dogged by difficulty
of making words take wings
did I want to be like the dog
skiving off through the paddock
up to no good – or was I just doggedly
doing the done thing – the expected
what was I up to – where was I up to
was I up to it – when the unexpected
letting go – losing my grip
joy – caught in a rip – how could I reject
how could I accept – strike dead
as a doornail a lifetime – or jam
myself into a box – if you stick a pig
it screams like a human – but he
was stunned into silence – we
came unstuck.

Home is broken
what words for the stickybeaks
what words for the children
what calendar
for no-longer-arriving future?

Break up – break open – heart-breaker
breakaway – tearaway
tear out the page

the dictionary says
stiction is static friction.

Station

Stationary lines move
all roads lead away

> I was naïve
> I hadn't understood
> I thought there was room.

This domed and gracious space
could be Waterloo or Victoria
an age when trains chugged
according to strict timetables
to stations that no longer exist

> I hoped one didn't
> have to choose
> I believed love had
> infinite capacity.

Please stand behind the yellow line!

> I hadn't figured out
> the daily necessities
> house-space   laundry   bills
> the grammar of marriage.

The lifts don't work
the disabled toilet's shut
I'm trying not to think
what everyone will think.
It's hard to manage a suitcase
and walk on crutches.

I remember the general confession

> *Forgive what we have been*
> *Amend what we are*
> *Direct what we shall be.*

The tracks run coolly
to and fro.

There's a moment
when seeking
has to freeze
into destination.

Uncertainty Principle

According to Heisenberg
an electron can't have precise position
and precise velocity; can't 'know'
where it is and where it's going.

I'm becoming someone I don't know
and possibly don't like.

I know nothing
but the brink of a cliff
harness chafing my shoulders
thin helmet, air, a leap.

Wordless

Some clauses fracture
language – my father
is dead, I have left
my husband.

Who is that woman
in the mirror, face never
seen before? Woman
who abandons thirty-five
years of the staid domestic

for the light fantastic.

Is it delayed adolescence?
is she so deeply loved?
does she love in return?
do the kisses know?

What will become of her?
does she care?
does it matter?

At the museum she winces
at the chains round
aboriginal necks

puts out a finger
flinches when a great white
leaps from behind the glass
to rip her arm off.

Here are insects frozen
in plastic, dinosaurs'
thick-limbed grace
extinct flick-knife claws.

Whispering foreign words
I am not a wife, she touches
the breast of the sea-eagle.

IV: Jarred

Jarred

A found poem

Nineteen-ninety-six
floods in Florence

the director of the Museum
escaping across the roofs
with Galileo's telescope

thousands of antique objects
destroyed or swept away

a trapped woman
in a wheelchair
drowning despite priests
reaching their arms
through the bars to lift her

horses locked in their stables
screaming and thrashing

half of Christ's side
and face stripped
from Cimabue's masterpiece

unimagined consequences

mud angels from all over Europe
washing the filth from cracked pots

book pages stuck to the ceiling
scholars wading through oily water
flaked with scraps of paint

picking over the broken pieces
reassembling the vestiges
of black paint on terra cotta
filling the gaps with clay
reforming the shape.

Michael Dirda, 'Art overwhelmed by nature', review of Robert Clark's *Dark Water: Flood and Redemption in the City of Masterpieces*, *Australian Financial Review*, 21.11.08.

Flat Earth

I've stepped off the edge of my life
a contortionist's tangled legs and arms flailing
the music of the spheres rude with shock
unwaxed feathers drifting down
onto flattened remnants of garden

I twist my neck to see
my crumpled limbs
through other people's telescopes
unbalancing profit and loss.

I knew but did not know the costs
could not pre-empt these doubts.

Peremptory love under spring boughs
bring me a cup of tea
kiss my cold shoulders and feet
tell me there's no rabbit trap
pressing into my skull

let your voice and fingers
keep speaking of the wild place
somewhere in the mountains
where sparks from a twilit bonfire
fly above these jagged slopes.

Auxiliaries

There were causes:

> I could be
> I have been
> I did, but
> I shouldn't

not to mention:

> he might have
> he wouldn't
> he was, but
> he couldn't

and also:

> we should have
> we didn't
> we tried, but
> we weren't

but these facts remain:

> I am not there
>
> I am here
>
> I will not be there when he hears

I live at the periphery of what used to be central

the Hume Highway is long

my back aches as much as my heart.

Unsettled

Today I dig up the grass
on the other side of the fence
wonder if the soil is suitable
for tomatoes

hang one mug
on the cup hooks
in your flat.

No job
no house
four books
no bookshelves
no paddock
a dog who is uncertain
if I may belong here.

I fill in a change-of-address form
cannot bring myself to unpack.

You've put my name with yours
on the answer machine

no friends ring me
no mail comes
my children speak
stiffly on the phone.

Though on the dance floor
with you in my arms
I feel a different rhythm
in the swing of my hips

the words I love you
depend for their truth
on the stability of the I.

Tricky Arithmetic

Irrational numbers cannot be expressed as a fraction

As summed integers
He and She had many
a tea-for-two, built a four-square
family, totted up
years of birthdays
and Christmas concerts
the exponential growth
of extended families

deaf to the hidden
subversive surds.

His apparent even-temperedness
his measure-three-times-cut-once
meticulous carpentry
and still-five boyishness counting out
the smarties after breakfast
masked some hidden corner
of doubt, baulking at a problem
in multiplication
He didn't know the factors for

while under her efficiency
was a restless energy
chain reactions that left
radioactive waste in the psyche
a charged ion seeking
its extra electron.

Two's a companionable coefficient
but when She started singing hymns
to Her, trying to triangulate
her path across chaos by the light
of seventy-times-seven
candles lit in every dark chapel

She passed, creeping step
by step across the gulf
on what She thought of as
the catena of prayer
She blinded herself to the obvious
that to work out the x in the quadratics
some of the elements have to swap sides.

She + He × by Her
= She ÷ by conflicting loyalties

1 + 1 in a new city
= who-knows-what
future possibilities
She × by Her
= She discovering herself
= two pairs of hands
playing four-part inventions
in what seems like
a parabola of grace.

But also there's the absurd notion
of incalculable square roots
the negative capability of grief:

She + Her = He - She
= 4 - 1 when the children visit
= He alone in the once-full house
night after night
the incongruent geometry
measuring the sullied earth
of others' loss.

Whatever strategies She applied
to this unforseen algebra
the numbers didn't stack up

where is integrity now?

Ordinary Time

I just want to be ordinary, you said.

>But what about when lambchopdom sets in?
>What? Two women in a kitchen?
>asked the doubting Thomasinas.

It's not the kitchen, it's crying at the washing line
>over the wrong pegs, different shops
>a strange dentist stuffing his fingers in my mouth
>and no small birds.

It's not the ordinary, there's no domestic rut
>there's New Year bouncing
>round the green by the storm-water drains
>dancing the Gay Gordons.

There's no problem at all with lamb-loin chops
>it's the old dog's hair in handfuls on the carpet
>and why can't you get out of bed?

Sometimes it's down-right greasy mutton
>bills, plumber, builder, dirty windows
>three new jobs
>three new logins
>all my addresses gone
>with the stolen laptop.

Nothing is ordinary
>   grandsons in Newcastle and Glenbrook
>   work in Canberra
>   funerals in Sydney
>   blood tests
>   my mother in hospital.

Eighty-eight days away in the first year
home somewhere along the Hume
two women in our kitchen would be a relief.

The dog dies
you get pneumonia
the curse of Icarus requires
that the builder go paragliding.

Christmas is hullabaloo
I'm obnoxious afterwards
but not in the kitchen
and anyway, so are you
but not for long.

Overall, there's no problem at all in the kitchen
and it's not always lamb chops
>   it's stuffed zucchini flowers
>   syllabub and angels on horseback.

Forty-two days away
before the first of March
sometimes I forget to miss you
until an unexpected ache from chest to midriff.

I express-post unnecessary messages
I'll overtake on the way home.

What the hell's wrong with lamb chops?

Responses

Those who don't answer letters
whose voices turn cold
refuse invitations

those simply thunderstruck
the old Italian friends we can't bear to tell
those who treat me like a snake

those who've withdrawn
what I thought was given
those whom I should no longer ring

and those who across generations
inconceivable boundaries
of Japanese or Muslim culture, say

you are my sister
you found you could not be yourself
you are my everlasting friend.

Infidelities

What my speech recognition program thinks I said

it's hopelessly out of date and uneducated
it's hopelessly out of lights

mortal sin, mournful scene

some months ago I wrote a poem
sun earth over a phone call

elegy for the church
energy for the church
allergy for the church
allergic to the church

flat choirs, flat clients
I became pious, I became pipes
organ pipes perhaps

I found a whole book, I found a cool book
it was the Bible, it was a vital, it was the viable

I started to think for myself, I found myself in it
of course the nuns wrung their hands
of course the nuns run hands
but my faith but my gay but my fair but my day but may fare

calm and unsullied
calm and I'm sailing

saved me from my house party, saved me from my excessive piety
suited me from my excess impiety

if I can't trust my friends
if I can't trust my prayers

no doubt he'd think I am a sinner
no doubt he'd think I am the centre

write the truest sentence you know
light through this sentence you know of

the grief eases a little
the grief years a little

V: Translated

Because

now my hands learn
things they never knew
they could do

because if you half-wake me
in the middle of the night
I can make complicated tender jokes

and it doesn't matter
if skin against skin leads
anywhere beyond simple rest

because skullduggery
is not in your dictionary.

Just My Cup of Tea

my hands cup
your shoulder, your breast
you teach me to savour
my own aromas
you stir all
the fluids within me
you know how
to make me
a perfect cup of tea

Effervescence

One Wednesday morning
        bubbles of joy
                float up

from the warm clay-pipe
of the city basin
      soar
            over the Brindabellas

the sky's grey pod has burst
      raining plenty
           of coloured peas

above down-on-earth workers
driven
along the Parkway
in our hasty carapaces.

No picnics by the lake for us
only a race
into the blue midweek
hot air balloons
a dangerous distraction
as we count
      a dozen
           fourteen
                seventeen

      silk teardrops drifting
            towards champagne breakfasts
                in free flow

while we slow woefully to forty

on the clogged-even-in-Canberra artery
almost afraid to look up
    at the yellow
        purple
            orange
    gumdrops glistening
        in the sky's bowl.

But work is no toad squatting on my life.

After a day of tiring my mind's hands
laying the stonework of confidence

teaching
    brown Namibian skin
        blue Finnish eyes
            boys from Chinese farms
                Saudis wearing hijab
to write about blood loss or web architecture

    bubbles of understanding
        floating up as we
            refine sentences
                about basalt
                      or sandstone regolith

I come home and you are wearing
    a red shirt
        cooking plenty of greens for my dinner.

Why I Still Go to Church

This moment
Which doesn't drift away.

> John Foulcher, 'Why I go to church'

Never for the flat parish choirs

sometimes for tea-towelled shepherds
and tinselled sleepy angels

possibly for the story of St Martin de Porres
who promised the rats he'd feed them
if they stopped annoying the prior

certainly not for the sermon that never asks
can Neanderthal men be saved?
can a single death two thousand years ago
redeem the hypothetical populations
of 55 Cancri's planets 41 light years away?

partly because even if no one is there
sometimes in the vaster spaces
of St Kit's, I feel a charged stillness
always because of the kneeling, the touch
of fingers on forehead, the taste of the host
the red, green, purple rhythm of seasons
wisdom of parables, music of psalms

now because of you kneeling beside me,
thumbing the scarred leather
of the little Mass book your grandmother
hid at the back of her Protestant linen press

and today because, driving up Canberra Avenue
when the national flagpole soars
like Lucifer above Parliament House
points to the Big Syringe
of modern communication on Black Mountain
aligns briefly with the spire of St Stephen's
it's the stone steeple that has human dimensions.

Found in Translation

My faithful fiddle
her corners my coin
rest on her bosom keeps me sane

her friendship my bark
her raisin my rhyme
my ravings settle in dreams beside her

her hands my mainstay
her back my dose
she is the arrow of my flesh

her hat a chapter
that I wear
she is the apple of my poem

the chance of my song
the jet of my fling
an oriole whistles in my ear

her heart a cur
I saved from the pound
I feel her foot upon my gown

I oil her brass
I stroke her chair
my horses gallop through her hair

our fur's on fire
our bed is lit
I knock upon her golden door

this peace our pay
our godly dew
we pry the ceiling with our prayers

her love my necessary birth
her death the terror of my earth.

Stolen Lines

Tempo rubato

So much depends upon
a thing so dark and deep
as the scattering of numbers
and yet our man of snow
may be, nonetheless, content

William Carlos William, 'The Red Wheelbarrow'
James McAuley 'Pieta'
Wislawa Szymborska 'Discovery'
Richard Wilbur, 'Boy at the Window'

Chapel in Languedoc

After the queues for the Vatican
the finger of God on a shopping bag
and a beggar with no arms outside

after the ancient priest at Badia
giving an inaudible homily
to children itching for their mobile phones

after Slovenia's shrines
in the corner of every field
and the churches empty on Sunday

we arrive where the Popes and Bishops
burned Cathars alive, cut children to pieces
Kill them all, God will know his own.

How can I still need this cracked edifice
this crippled hierarchy?

Something prompts us to run
to Mass in the tiny broken chapel
held up by the brutal force of concrete columns.

Here's a statue of Sainte Germaine
whose distaff in the ground protected
her sheep from the wolves as she went to mass.

Here women to whom this means everything sing
a young Romanian priest with fluent gestures
fetches his dog into church for the last hymn.

Here on this sunny hill where wild oats
blow over the once bloody plain
is this rough-stone lopsided chapel
with ancient frescoes, almost effaced.

If

if grammar is the ground of all
if meaning is in the gaps
if my breathing alters, you know why

if neutrinos pass through our lungs and liver, unnoticed
if we'd never laughed together
if one word acts as an arch to the next

if my breathing alters you, alters the pace of yours
if meaning is the white space surrounding the line
if some old fear in you has flickered

if god exists
if our prayers are more than words' dry leaves flying up
from a bonfire of debris
if words are blocks of thought mortared with syntax

if conditionals are of two kinds, possible and impossible
if we'd met earlier, even one day, even an hour

Depth of Field

in my Leica binoculars
bought on the Rue de Rivoli
new eyes with depth of field
detailed clarity of raindrops
branch, node, sprig, leaf

an air-spout out to sea
humpbacks with calves
heaving their vast bulk
out of the quiet waves
numbers recovering

godwits lift from the flats
and wheel above
little terns whitter
hang in the air
on fluttering wings

three years since I came to you –
the sky, the water, the evening
a squadron of cormorants overhead
tiny red-capped plovers scuttling
across the sand at the brink of the lake.

Whatness

If you want to say that 'God is energy,'
then you can find God in a lump of coal.

Stephen Weinberg

What lump of coal
what latent fire
what nothingness
what thisness
what neverness
what isness

what polarity
what push or pull
stability or risk
adventure, cost
what gain what loss
what abstract giving rise
to thingness

what pasts what memories with him
what children wanting to be born
and born of us

what plantings
what tomorrowings with her
what visits, visitations

what pomegranate
what red wheelbarrow
found at the tip
what future action
may depend on it

what hope of one-day stillness.

Code to Found in Translation

faithful: fidele
corner: le coin
bosom: le sein
ship: la barque
reason: le raison
dream: la rêve
hand: le main
back: le dos
hat: le chapeau
apple: la pomme
song: la chanson
fling: jeter
ear: l'oreille
heart: le cœur

fuck: foutre
cunt: le con
arm: le bras
flesh: la chair
horses: les chevaux
hair: les cheveux
fire: le feu
bed: le lit
golden: d'or
peace: la paix
god: Dieu
pray: prier
birth: la naissance
earth: la terre

www.ingramcontent.com/pod-product-compliance
Lightning Source LLC
Chambersburg PA
CBHW070323120526
44590CB00017B/2800